404 Not Found
by Lucas Baisch

53 SP 47

May 2024
Brooklyn, NY

404 Not Found
© Lucas Baisch 2024
53rdstatepress.org

ISBN Number: 979-8986581439
Library of Congress Number: 2024931606

Book design: Nathan Baron Silvern
Cover design: Jonathan Herrera Soto

Printed on recycled paper in the United States of America.

404 Not Found is made possible by the New York State Council on the Arts with the support of the Office of the Governor and the New York State Legislature.

404 Not Found
by Lucas Baisch

53rd State Press
Brooklyn, NY

Contents

Introduction

I'm sitting on the Amtrak reading this play again. In front of me is a pale guy in a gray suit who's been on his phone talking business since New Rochelle. "Well," he says after a pause, "to make a long story long..." He's got a kind of singsong salesman voice, tenor, running up the scale and back down into fake-conspiratorial fry:

"We can prolly yank that, right?"

Right, right.

"You can't like, front an RSA. Right?"

Right, of course, that'd be...

"I hate to disappoint you, but, we're gonna have to shut down yer lil project. Kay?"

Ok, that last line isn't something the guy says. It's a line from *404 Not Found* by Lucas Baisch, the play you're about to read, or already read, or maybe deciding if you should read (you definitely should). The point I'm making is that the power and desperation that saturate the real, every-day world are always seeping into language and deforming it, making it unbearable, a screech in your ear, making you want to double over and stick your head all the way into the poem you've got open in front of you. If that poem is one of Lucas's plays, though, the joke's on you, because the "claw hand, / Dragging across metal" is in there too. The poem, the dream, the fantasy is no escape. After all, it's in the dream that Freddy Krueger gets you. But if he's all around us anyway, don't you wanna look him in the face? Maybe in the intimacy of that clinch you too can "become a thing of nightmares. / You become a thing of—" Anyway it's worth a try.

I remember feeling something of this hope when Lucas first sent me pages from this play in June of 2020. I had moved to Providence from New York to run the Brown MFA Playwriting program a few months earlier; Lucas graduated from the program that spring. Somewhere in between my coming and his going, the world had ground to a halt, and now we were both stuck in Rhode Island, possibly forever. We sat masked in a grassy square called (cruelly, I thought) Prospect Park. Life had become sharply unreal. I tried to convey to Lucas how good this play's ruthless world-warping felt in that moment. I probably didn't say that the characters he'd written made me less lonely, though that was also true.

404 Not Found turns reality inside-out, over and over, Möbius-style. Obviously it's about capitalism, about the underworlds on which our overlords depend. It's also about ingenuity, about the wild shit people come up with in order to keep going. Every one of the three characters is a genius. First there's Slack, heartthrob torturer, who pries out teeth and then pries open time portals, burns up his whole wretched world for the sake of an abstract thrill. He's making hash browns in his toaster oven one day when a shoebox full of teeth—his victims'?—shows up in his kitchen, propelling him into a strangely barren outside. He starts driving, and eventually he stops to pick up two other wanderers.

One of them is Ro, who's stolen her grandma's pension and faked her own death. She figures out how to make ends meet by dressing up as Krueger for traumatized truckers. Ro is the most relentless person we meet. Unlike the other two characters, her desire never really finds an object, a project to invest; her energy is channeled into survival and her libido surges towards nothingness, emptiness, wild negation. This makes me want to claim that Lucas is actually using Ro to help us imagine who Freddy would be on the inside: that despite appearance, Ro is Freddy K turned inside-out—which actually lines up pretty well if we rephrase it as: Freddy with the seams showing.

The third character is Ro's "kid cousin" Cameo, who's engineered an online world called La Barranca (The Ravine)—a simulated jungle landscape where asylum-seekers can find the documents they need for real-life immigration. "Abuelita used to call him 'papa sin sal,'" Ro reminisces, "and I felt bad cuz people mistook him for boring, shrimpish, when on the inside, he's actually psychotic." Well, everyone in this play is psychotic, because that's what the world is (our world, I mean, not La Barranca). But Cameo is the world-builder; he's the playwright, I think, and personally I picture him as Lucas, even though—refusing, whew, the confessional moment that's now the norm of American play-writing—he never comes out and says so.

Partners in crime, the cousins get picked up by Slack, who probably intends to use them as human fuel for his time-travel project. They keep driving south until they find themselves "in the forest highlands of an undisclosed Central American country," which is when and where the play begins. Or is it? The more we hear from the characters in their monologues, the more it starts to seem like we might actually all be inside La Barranca—but a fucked-up version of it that's been rewired, colonized by the guy sitting in front of me on the Amtrak, a shadowy figure who shows up inside Cameo's simulation and spooks him into shutting it down. "I've pulled the plug," he muses. "Everything drawn up as blank. / You erase yourself. / A web page reading: 404 Not Found."

Don't worry, though—that's not the end. In fact, even the end isn't really the end. "I might be able to undo some things, right? Right?"

Right?

—Julia Jarcho

Setting

There is a clay wall, outside-facing, painted hospital scrub, greenish-blue.

Its top: lined with broken glass bottles and barbed wire.

Flakes of plastic-bag caught between them.

There is a metal grate over a square window.

There is a man handcuffed to its bar.

Characters

SLACK - [he/him] mid 30s
withered, wicked, time travelling.
mixed ('mestizo') Mexican-American.

RO - [she/her] late 20s to early 30s
in Freddy Krueger cos-play.
Guatemalan-American.

CAMEO - [he/him] early 20s
kid cousin. potential techie in training.
Guatemalan-American.

Maybe the only way to do this play
Is if you've stayed awake
For seven days straight.

"You can only possess what is immovable. And time is what cannot be apprehended, continuous change and fleetingness. A culture arrives at the idea of spatialized time, of a progress of time that builds monuments, that colonizes becoming itself by affixing historical touristic plaques in its wake, that colonizes when it cannot confront death, when it is guarding against oblivion. Time is the enemy of the empire."

—Heriberto Yépez,
The Empire of Neomemory

"Let evil explode on the stage, show us naked, leave us haggard, without recourse except in ourselves. It's not the function of artists to find practical solutions for evil. Let the artists accept damnation. They may lose their soul, if they have one. That doesn't matter. But their work must be an explosion to which people will react as they can."

—Jean Genet,
by way of my friend & teacher Lisa D'Amour

"I forgot how much it hurts to be human."

—Freddy Krueger
Freddy's Dead: The Final Nightmare

1. SPIT AND SWALLOW

> SLACK *is cuffed to the metal grate window.*
>
> *His other arm – in a sling.*
>
> *An obscured figure enters.*
>
> *He holds a red solo cup to* SLACK*'s mouth.*

CAMEO
Drink.

> SLACK *drinks the contents of the cup,*
>
> *Holds the liquid. Swirls.*

CAMEO
Spit.

> SLACK *spits.*

CAMEO
All of it.

> *All of it.*
>
> *The figure looks in the cup, checks his watch.*

CAMEO
Good.

The figure exits.

SLACK, *in a shock of light:*

SLACK
For years, talking to myself, I'd say, 'Meet me
at the toaster oven.' Walk my ass to the kitch-
en pantry, dripping wet from the shower. Daily.
Number three. Depressive. Stick two frozen hash
browns in the bear trap, watch it heat up orange,
turn the browns all black, all charred, then chow
down. A dasha soy sauce, garlic powder – I'm
wretched. But this go-round at the ole toast and
slobber, this time, we pull an emergency brake.
My midnight monotony, shift-gear-reverse.

'Christ now, how'd that get here?' I blink at a
paper package on the floor, damp at the corner. Vinegar blotches? Guess I thrash a bit. Ya
pick it up, unravel the twine, turkey yer fingers
'round it, shake it a little, jingle. This is a shoebox. And when I rip off its lid – this is a coffin.
Inside, teeth. Human teeth. Incisors, canine,
shades of grey and yellow, adult and child, teeth,
hundreds. Beads to be strung up like a damn
necklace. Worn like a badge for something cul-

tish. 'Where and why?' I putter, 'Where. Why.'
It's worrisome. And I'm disgusted. With my own
lack of surprise, 'specially considering I hadn't
received package in months, perhaps a year, and
here a crusty shoebox shows up on my linoleum
– I didn't put it there. I did not ask for this.

So, I'll send a text to Crowley. Nico Crowley.
Crowbar. That's what we'd call him in grade
school, then correctional. Crowbar. As if a name
like that meant brutal or prying, when in reality
he's the softest boy. A jello spigot. Years later,
we keep on. He becomes a part of the family.
And presently, at kitchen shoebox, I'll send a
text. 'You leave this at the dining room table?' A
picture, for reference. A message error, the file
too big, my data run out, poor connection – his
service?

Crowley, Crowbar, Crowley. Years ago he'd
saved my brother from a suicide mission. Found
his frothy mouth passed out in a closet, stuck up
one-uh those road homes the two of 'em rented
from a senile family friend. This old bag, sweet
woman. Crowbar heaves my brother upright, sits
him inna plastic chair, no phoning the police,
never phoning the police. Takes it upon himself

to flood the system. A pop uh Narcan and we're back in business.

We weren't friendly us two, my brother 'n me. We made Crow less so. We quickly graduate from petty theft to breaking and entering to – well, other things. Cuz in the Central Valley – California – that skinny little middle part folks forget about – no lustful oceanside, no forest sprawl –. there's only ten to twelve ways to be. The majority involve being ruthless. And whose cross is it to bear when a miscreant turns to prof-it? I'd say everyone's, probably.

We kidnap a pansy boy. We drive him in the back of Crowbar's pick up, bungee cord him to a recliner. Wedge a bitta steel wool in his mouth 'cause he'd done the boys dirty. An abandoned parking structure, all fenced in. Wire cutters. A break in the chainlink. Band-Aids on each finger cuz we broke 'em with a mallet. I catch a glimpse of the poor kid's chest hairs floating out his button-up, ingrown, stubby red, growing back from a self-shearing. Like he knew he was destined to be a lamb, God's lamb. My arm's in a sling, so I can't help much, but I watch my brother and Crowbar and I'm smacking gum –

it's cinnamon. The two of 'em step away and kid says, 'Look man. You've got the wrong Rita.'

'Hold on boys, hold a second.' I make some jest. 'Maybe we should – maybe we could – *let him go?*' We burst out laughing. The three of us. Some holier than thou garble – I'm kidding. I'm joking. I'm nauseous.

My brother has Crowley take the car keys from ignition. He tries to back out, and I say, 'push on.' And. Well. We wedge out every molar. Every wisdom bite, one by one, and baby Rita goes spitting blood up my pant leg. Cawing on, gums flaring. Slaaaaam dunk. He looks small. Particularly small. Like old man small. Shrink wrap. Me, tough guy, I skip outta there pretending to take a piss, when really I'm blowing chunks. Profuse. Ashamed. Alone. Frozen bile crusted on my sneaker, and we never talk about it again.

Fast forward and I win a mystery shoe box. Shit. I don't hear from Crowley-Crowbar after message error. He doesn't wanna talk to me after I – he's – he isn't answering my texts, my emails, my phone calls, because I think he got the tooth necklace too. Won the package. Kitchen floor. The problem is, he put it on. Regalia. Death dressage. Everyone did. And when I make my way outside, into an empty public, I notice no one's there. I make my journey into a desert, a neo-Jesús, everything Judean, all of us one sexy, sick Judas, pining for the next person to make toothless.

And I – like you – end up here. At a trench in the mountain. Wire cutters. A break in the chainlink and this freakish family found me. Or maybe I found them. They stapled a placard to my chest. They gave me a new name. They call me 'History.' That's the top-off. Upon my arrival, like I'm a second-coming and not some local ingrate. 'History.' All-in-one. Jackpot, whack a mole, the crane game caught me. 'History.' *(Laughing.)* I'ma fuckin' sentient tree ring, but the knotty kind. Knotty like knots. Mangled branch, that's me. I'm fixed to a window grate, getting my ass wiped by her and him and they leave me a plastic cuppa water. They put a rock in it, so the wind won't take it away.

There's wind here. Ya feel it?

There's wind here.

Do you feel that? The wind means ritual means a place needs repairing. Deliverance. A box of tooth jewelry. Time travel.

The sound of boots on gravel.

Someone unseen.

You still there? Someone there? Ya gonna help me outta here or – or – you, uh – are you some – some – some parta all that sideways logic?

Ah?

2. THE COCHINA ANTHEM

RO *sets a folding chair, some distance away.*

Horror movie theme.

Something like Elm Street.

She applies make-up.

She's dressed as Freddy K.

RO

This is how you fake your own death. You make friends with someone savvy in computer magic. You have 'em forge a death certificate, stolen, signed from a county coroner. The accident report of a fatal blank, two bodies found *blank*, names: *blank* and *blank*. You get someone to cosign on a dummy-body. Identify it as you. All you. You never stage a funeral. Never look yourself up. You make yer footprint the size of an infant, then a mouse, then a specka nothing-dust. And if yer naturalized, it won't matter much. Because they never saw you as natural. The word 'legal' is a drunken catcall. Nah. The most natural thing they saw was hurricane season. You as mudslide, as loud-loud, as chanclas y berrinches, 'así, quieres pow-pow,' as a cleaner girl lookin' to get clean when I never cleaned a thing in my goddamn life. You grab yourself, your only family – in my case, one child idiot – then blanket your bodies in the back of a big rig. Auto transport. The back seat of the very back car. Lazy truckers won't find you there.

This is how you fake your own death.

This is the anthem of your favorite cochina.

You make your way down south, hanging out at rest stops. You get roped into being a *lot lizard*. Mistress of the eighteen-wheelers, all on accident, all with tact. Bored truckers, looking for a toilet greaser, the only ones to think I'm sexy, and it's less about sexy, not about sex at all, more about – um. *(Smirks.)* Look at me. Every day I'm Freddy Krueger. A truck driver, big guy, hairy fuck – he likes me red in the face, and I like the penny in his pocket. He says Nightmare, I say Elm Street. The guy – Hairy Gary – he wound up reeling from some arson trauma, a teenager, said his parents passed away in a house fire, burning. He dresses up in his best Nancy Thompson, horror heroine, costumed like schoolgirl. Permed wig, five o' clock shadow. He buys me prosthetics. Blade hands. A hat. I leave my cousin in motel parking lots and Hairy Gary sets his camcorder 'cross from me. We don't touch each other. He cries himself to sleep.

You switch vehicles and Hairy Gary gives you a ride down the 99. He drops you off and keeps your contact. He haggles your content, has you send him videos, applying costume in exchange for cash. Envelopes in secret, escorted through a rest stop courier service – the footprint: ghostly. Hairy Gary understands your commitment to becoming unknown. He respects you and he respects your cause. Hairy Gary. Fake Nancy.

Y'know, I knew this bitch named Nancy once. Used to make funna the beans Abuelita'd pack me for lunch. Call 'em shit beans. Call me shit-mouth. Well, my shit-mouth turns to a shit-fist, and knuckles meet a jawbone. And then I get suspended. And then me n' my girl Ampi go carve skid donuts into the parking lot with her uncle's low-rider.

The high-pitched screech and squeal of burning rubber in orbit. Hydraulic pump, rickshaw car frame, bustling like yer brother in bunk bed, post-virginal, post-sixty-second homecoming fuck. I oughtta fall out the window, I think. Rolled all the way down, seatbelt all the way off – wanting that same pull toward an ether, crossing county lines and, the back of the big rig, the back of Hairy Gary's road-kennel, window rolled all the way down for me to fall into. Out to. Out with.

A grim bliss shudders from above:

CAMEO, *in shadow.*

CAMEO
Who's there?

RO
A torso trashed against a metal wall.

CAMEO
Ro, I think he's bleeding.

RO
Put him in the trunk.

CAMEO
I can't pick him up, he's too heavy, he's –

RO
We'll take his car.

CAMEO
His arm's all fucked.

RO
Pick him up!

CAMEO
Ro, I told you, I can't!

RO
(To audience.) My kid cousin makes me awkward by proxy. Abuelita used to call him 'papa sin sal,' and I felt bad cuz people mistook him for boring, shrimpish, when on the inside, he's actually psychotic.

CAMEO, *in other light.*

CAMEO
How many times do I have to fucking tell you –

RO
You spitta 'nother word like that, I rip yer tongue out.

CAMEO
Do I have to fucking SAY –

RO
Cállate la boca, YA?

CAMEO
you would be fucking ruined without me ungrateful ungrateful ungrateful i never – you never – we never –

RO
What's that?

CAMEO
–

RO
(To audience.) The lyric to my cochina anthem:

(To CAMEO.*)* MY FAVORITE SEX POSITION IS THE HEIMLICH MANEUVER. IT'S THE WAY I TRAIN MY ARM UP YOUR CLAVICLE. CHOKE, THEN UN-CHOKE AWAY. YOU ARE THE THING STUCK IN MY THROAT, CAMEO – now we good or we good?

> *A headlight passes over everyone.*
>
> *A car door opens and slams.*
>
> *Someone holds a flashlight up to* RO, CAMEO.
>
> *It traces over them, frozen.*
>
> *No one moves.*
>
> *Boots on gravel.*
>
> *No one moves.*
>
> *Boots on gravel.*

A car door opens and slams.

They drive away.

Bodies relax.

CAMEO
Hey.

RO
Sorry, I'm –

CAMEO
(Joking, sheepish.) I was a jerk before. I went back to my corner and I started to hate myself. I hate myself a bit. Do you forgive me?

RO
I'm busy now, / I've gotta –

CAMEO
Great. Can I have one-uh the freezie dinners? The boxes in the cooler?

RO
Sure. Fine. Take whatever.

CAMEO
Sick. That's real sick.

CAMEO *disappears.*

RO

In faking your own death you have to change
your name.

Veronica   Guadalupe   Amezquita   Villacruz.
Carved at a dreamscape epitaph. A grave marker,
which never stood the chance to exist, because
erasure is the standard and Ro is easy. Ro sounds
like white boy. I'ma white boy now. I wobble
down the street with the hanging nutsack of
a trust fund. The song of machismo. Inherent
escape.

In faking your own death you curry favors from
strangers. You become una cochina fuerte. You
drink yer coffee, keeping yourself awake, alive,
moving in reverse, you keep the coffee on, Nes-
café, an electric boiler plate, hot plate, that cheap
shit tasting like gold, and the plate's a makeshift
space heater, and heat's the only goal.

In faking your own death you become a thing of
nightmares.

You become a thing of –

SLACK
'Hey. Y'all need a ride?'

3. LA BARRANCA GOES LIVE

A high-pitched squeal-laugh.

CAMEO *eats a dinner freezie.*

A train of red solo cups tied to his belt.

CAMEO
And three, two, one.
A space bar means the death of me.
And I am *yoked* on this shit, bro.

I open for you a canyon, sliced betweena jungle canopy. Inside this canyon: some Hype. Ass. Shit. We gotta village. A greenhouse. A garden, a school. Beside this village is a dried out creek bed. I've put a sign up. I call it: La Barranca. I'm seeking a thing of salvation. Cuz when you make yourself dead, you've gotta have a place to go. The trick – La Barranca is a digital landscape. Borders I've built in binary. A place where passports are shoved into bedrock and nation-state means nothing. Built it myself. Nothing hard, ya see I'm quick. A country of my own design, where I've tethered myself to a mobile router.

Look.

He lifts up his shirt.

We see a router haphazardly tied to his torso.

I put it onna public server with the intention of utopia. You know that word? Utopia? Safe house? Refuge? Made it for access. A meeting point for those seeking communion, encrypted, anonymous. The relocated lookin' to reconnect, simulate some socializing, fill in their blanks. Maybe someone needs a document to tack to themselves. In La Barranca, I've engineered placards aplenty.

A ding. The ticker goes up. Someone's online. A customer? Ro's in a rest stop bathroom, filming make-up tutorials for Hairy Gary, and I'm crouched between a shrub and a brick wall, laptop fan running. I type in the chat: 'Hello?' No response. Huh.

So I keep on, terraforming my plot while I listen to the police scanner. I build a cliff. A mine. A mountain range. Ten fourteen means suspicious person. A four fifteen – 'disturbance.' A two oh seven's kidnap. Then a ding. A message. White lettering in the monitor. Eyes all squinty. *What's that say? (Reading.)* 'Suck my dick.' Frickin' cricket-shit, bro – 'Yo, if yer not here to pick up, I could just boot you. I could – ' An ellipses. They're typing. A double-down. 'I said: Suck. My. Dick.'

(*Laughs.*) Ya gonna come at me then say it with yer whole CHEST, bro. You wanna play? I can play. My faggotry licks at the keyboard. A code crack is a dick suck is adrenaline rush, coursing through my Diet Coke drudgery, my typing wrists. And I'm no architect urban design bachelor master graduate savant. No, I am idiot. On that doo-doo brain, then sideswipe 'em with my cunning, my skill, with surprise finesse. I give the cricket-shit a soft warning.

'Look man, yer wasting yer time. I could ruin you. Scrounge up an IP, peer into yer bank account, yer search history, pull yer social security, weed out yer most wicked, yer most *horrid* – '

'No.' They cut me off.

'That's not what we're doing, Cameo.' The police scanner. A ten fourteen. A four fifteen. The sound of the neighboring freeway. 'I know what you've built. You got a bitta gold embedded in that creek there, don'tcha? Some sorta itch for charity? Tell me, what do you see right now?

In real life.' *Real life.* I peek over the shrubbery. Make some shit up. 'I see – uh – a lady mowing her lawn. Some neighbor walking dog. A kid doin' chalk doodles.' In *Real Life* – a radio signal. Dispatch one through fifty. A siren.

> *The sound of a squad car in the distance.*

'You're lying. What do we do with liars, brother? How do we deal with fibber-boys? You're at a rest stop. You see a gas station 'cross the barricade.' Fuck. Someone's gotta tick on me, a tracker, FUCK. Ro's gonna be pissed, she'll make me – the cricket-shit trucks on: 'A man in his underwear limps into sight. He stops at the diesel pump holding a cardboard box.' Shit me not, they must've hooked up to some security cam cuz there's our dude, in the distance, tighty whiteys, limping blind into the open. A squad car pulls up. Then two. Three. Cops all over.

My unsolicited friend types in cypher: 'You are going to watch a man die.' Between my view of a digital jungle and a growing stand-off, I begin to feel my stomach turn over. Discord in the belly. The man is my avatar.

> SLACK *lights up, still cuffed to the window.*

CAMEO
I move him left.

> SLACK *sludges left.*

CAMEO
I move him forward.

> *He leans forward.*

CAMEO
I lift his hand. Make him smile. He crouches at shrubbery, a mirror of mine. Hands duck in. A shotgun wrapped in a towel, wrapped in a bush. The pig-shits are squealing. Don't shoot. Don't. Shoot.

Another ding. A message. 'Meet me at the clay house. The one painted greenish-blue, hospital scrub, barred windows. We'll make a deal.' Now that's the shit, man, that's the raucous *shit*. It's a locked building system. I didn't make no clay house in La Barranca. Someone's intercepted and they're typing:

'Duck.'

> *A shotgun fires.*

CAMEO *drops his dinner freezie.*

SLACK *goes away.*

I peek outta my covering and there's nothing. No tighty whitey, no squad cars, no shotgun. La Barranca is buzzing. *(Typing, but not typing.)* 'Who. Are. You?' My fingers feel away from me. 'I'm you. Mestizo boy. A colonial wound. A dog left to starve.' They exit server and I'm wildin'.

Tcht.

Psh.

Ffff.

'I ain't no frickin' colonial wound, *man*. I'ma scar. Healed over. War wound. Cut me with that backwash – *mestizaje* – pah. You keep on with this shit I'll source your location, make you real sorry.' Then a blip. A flag marker. I zoom in on my map, facing south, and the most vile thing: a small man is resurrected in my monitor. Underwear. Limping. He's holding a – what is that? A cardboard box. He's staring at me. He's grinning. I shake out of it. A streak of my hair's gone white.

RO *enters.*

Downs a cup of coffee,

Styrofoam crunch.

RO
I'm done now. We have to go.

She disappears.

CAMEO
La Barranca is open for occupation.

We host ten to twelve ways for you to dissoci-
ate. Zip line. Farm till. Message board. Grave.
Embedded in the creek, I practice something
haunted. And though I built the whole thing for
passage – to help people – honest – a community
can turn to leeching, and a web friend can be a
Nazi, and a plot can be tilled for resource, and
I'm scared they've got me now. Awful scared.

4. LEGO MOUTH

> CAMEO *sits in the folding chair.*
>
> *He plays some game-device.*
>
> *He and* SLACK *hold for a second.*

CAMEO
And Rita-boy – ?

SLACK
Uhp, uhp, uhp. Shh! Ya hear that?

There's something –

> *They listen.*

SLACK
You didn't hear that?

CAMEO
(Still playing game.) Keep going.

SLACK
Rita-boy's crying then humming then crying again. We took him from that fenced-in lot, drove him out to Crowbar's. We got him whimpering in a kiddie pool out back, all dried out, crusty tree leaves, tobacco spit. The chew –

> *He smells it.*

– stuck up 'gainst the plastic siding, smells like rubber, smells like burning, gunking up Rita's open wounds, a caulk for his holes. I say caulk like caulk, y'know, sealant? Filler? Not cock like dick like prick like – *pervert.* We're not touching the boy. Not like that, I mean. You get it. You got me. So. Rita's moaning toothless, and we start to shave his head. I realize, just under the base, under the back of his skull, the bulk of where his hair is, where we'd buzzed offa knotted rat tail – there's a hole. Skin fused up 'n round the gaping – like a crater, a planter's wart, or just some fuckin' hole, and part of me wants to fish my finger innit. Perfect size. Horny thumb.

CAMEO
You tell yer brother all that?

SLACK
My brother? Why would I tell my brother?

Why would you ask if I told my brother?

CAMEO
–

SLACK
I make note. I keepa secret. Kid won't keep quiet. Give him a packa antihistamines, try to get him to sleep, but he still makes noise. Putta

Band-Aid on top to match his broken fingers.
Stuff a lil Kleenex inside, wet with rubbing alco-
hol. Keeps it from – I don't know. Infection?
Infecting?

CAMEO
Benevolent.

SLACK
What's that?

CAMEO
You're soft. Spineless. All kind.

SLACK
Less kindness, more cowardly, more – aaaah, yer
fuckin' me up. My story. Yer making / all this
noise, and I'm just – I'm just tryna –

CAMEO
/ I'm sorry I'm sorry I'm sorry I'm –

> *The sound of boots on gravel.*
>
> *They perk.*
>
> CAMEO *checks his watch.*
>
> *He prepares a cup.*

CAMEO

The hole. You stuffed it. You sealed it. You caulked –

SLACK

I didn't caulk, just bandage, I, uh – my brother 'n Crowbar make me water boy. Kinda like yer my water boy. I like it. I get into it. We develop this rapport. Nighttime conversations perkin' up from his moans and my sentence. Whole chats, whole hangouts, midnight therapy pushin' til dawn.

CAMEO
Drink.

> CAMEO *holds the red solo cup to* SLACK's *face.*

SLACK

He arouses me. I don't know why, but it's – he's –

> SLACK *drinks.*

CAMEO
Spit.

> SLACK *spits.*

SLACK

So day fifteen or twenty or thirty whatever, Rita's
gotten loopy. He gives in to his – predicament.
He shifts his hips around. He wants to tell me
something, clearly. But, of course, we've been
pretty interpretive up 'til now, given his wonky-
tonk tooth-to-tongue ratio. I get this idea.

CAMEO

Pen 'n paper.

SLACK

WOULD YA LISTEN ALREADY? This is the
part, the most important part, and you asked –
you asked and I'm – ya keep cuttin' through with
yer –

> CAMEO *indicates a lip seal zip ges-*
> *ture.*
>
> *He stares into the plastic cup, lis-*
> *tening.*

SLACK

I'm scrambled eggs. My memory, it's all –

CAMEO

–

My brother's always been one to keep his old things. Tools and toys and gadgets and *stuff*, buckets of *stuff*. We got these little plastic building blocks all over the road home. Stepping on 'em. You'd think a kid lived there. A baby kid. At this point, Rita-boy's braying and Crowley says it's my problem, and I feel for the pansy, ya know. I have a heart. Even if it's this twisty backwards kinda sympathy-pity heart. So, I catch an idea. I don't feel guilty 'bout this part, 'cause this part – it's mercy. I go inside. I grab a handful of strewn about blocks. Legos. You know Legos? Those and a hot glue gun from the old bag's sewing basket.

I, um – I have Crowbar hold him down. His mouth ain't that big, so I pick out the smallest pieces. 'It's for helping. I'm here to help.' He shoots me this look like, 'Fuck me, I barely gotta choice, uh?' The glue gun is like cauterizing. Doctors do it. Couldn't be too far off, yeah? I get four, five pieces in, just up the front, keepin' his mouth a bit too open. Just enough for him to lick out a coupla words.

A jigsaw smile. Threads of glue and blood and mouth sore and plastic yellow, plastic blue – but he can talk. He's kind of – handsome. He's passed out. Coupla days fold over. He sticks to fetal position. Quiet now. Shaming me with his silence. Shits himself in the kiddie pool. I change him. I wash him. I feed him. He changes. I'ma caregiver now. I heat him up – toaster oven – soft bits of leftover pizza mush, hash brown, and he comes to. He wants to tell me his secrets.

He's had to relearn the alphabet. Figure out where syllables make meaning. A real embarrassment of riches when it comes to the time I spend sitting, waiting, clipping finger nails, watching my captive like a friggin' TV program. Season one watching episode repeats 'til season two, when my buddy, my pansy, my social experiment pulls on through.

CAMEO
What's 'aroused'?

SLACK
Huh?

CAMEO
Aroused. You said aroused before.

SLACK
You kidding?

CAMEO

I mean, I know what you mean, but only kind of, only like –

SLACK

Arousal's like – you ever pick a fresh flower? Cut the stems?

CAMEO

'Flower.'

SLACK

When the music resolves. When the clouds part. Christ, you're thick.

CAMEO

The kid, the kiddie pool –

SLACK

Right. Right so. Toy-teeth makes language. And for some reason the kid looks bigger than before. He babbles off and it takes me a bit to realize he's recounting dreams. *His dreams.* Says they must be telling him 'bout his waking life. Of course it sounds more like fish blubber, sounds like slop noise, but I come to understand he wants me to do something. He points to an old shed we have in the corner of the yard. A part where paint's begun to pull up from a side of the wall.

He tells me, 'ITH THUH COH-NUH.' It's the corner? Shakes his head. 'ITH. THUH. COH. NUH.' Itch. Itch. He's sayin' itch. Itch the corner. He wants me to go up to it. Nudge the edge of the shed with my fingernail. Why? He says he did it in a dream. A dream. He said it let him venture backwards. Forwards. He suggests some shit like time travel. Now, I've done plentya acid trip-goomba-shroom cap bullshit, I have a wide tolerance for people's spiritual visitations, but for some reason I'm gettin' so fuckin' hot in this moment, my face, my fists, so pissed off, all that work for – he wants me to stick my finger inna shed. Says I'll slip through time? A portal? The fuck's that gotta do with me, huh?

And I look at him. He isn't moving. He's staring at me, dead-on. He is chapped and he is metal. Rot iron lips screeching: 'Kiss me, kiss me,' when all I can think about's his flappy gums, his blood-stained tongue, licking at his salt wounds. Desperate. Makin' up science fiction. A whole discarded Lego. Yellow. A match.

CAMEO
Match?

SLACK

I hold up a match. I say, 'A thing can burn out real fast,' but threats mean nothing to the guy. Rita's five hundred pounds and his ingrown chest hairs are full of wolf hide and I'm kinda scared, I guess, not really, but a bit, and he presses. He says,

CAMEO
'Go on.'

SLACK
He says,

CAMEO
'Try it.'

SLACK

–

CAMEO
'Rip up the old bits at the base. You'll find a hole inside, like the one in the back of my skull. You'll like it there. I promise.'

SLACK
– he says the whole thing, just like that. He speaks complete idea now, perfect speech, and my anger-heat, it's getting hotter, I feel a bit woozy, weak-knee'd, fevers, itching, and I'm

walking across an overgrown lawn, hypnotized,
full daylight, to pick at a piece of metal.

> *The scratch of a shed's siding.*

SLACK
Horny thumb.

Horny hole.

I'm here.

Fingers at the ready.

Boom.

Whiplash.

Slop it up.

I've gone away.

CAMEO
What happens?

SLACK
Like something's exploded. Like he offered.
Time travel.

> CAMEO *drops the cup full of spit.*

CAMEO
Shit.

SLACK
Clumsy guy.

CAMEO
I'm sorry I'm sorry I'm sorry I'm –

SLACK
Rita-boy showed me.

CAMEO
Showed you –

SLACK
Imagine fallout. Moldy everything. And I'm still there by the toaster oven. It was incredible. No, no, it *will* be – incredible.

CAMEO
I'm –

–

–

SLACK
The mechanic, the shed-hole, the access to a skull hole – none of that's supposed to be 'blessed.' It's not – I'm not *chosen*. I'm not chosen 'cause I choose to get all vicious in my pastime. I'm no provider, I'm not saving anyone. If anything, I'ma cousin of something rotted. Like, I'm fuckin' evil, right? How the hell else did I end up – did you end up –

CAMEO
Shut up.

> CAMEO *pulls another solo cup off his belt.*
>
> *He fills it with some indiscernible liquid,*
>
> *And shoves it in* SLACK's *face.*

CAMEO
Again.

> SLACK *doesn't budge.*

CAMEO
I'll – I'll, uh,

I'll decipher the things you get to do –

And, and, and *maybe*

We can lengthen your slack – and *maybe* we can – maybe it's –

It's based on the flakes in the wash, okay? *Okay?*

Gotta make sure your mouth is clean,

Because my mouth has to stay clean.

Ro's mouth has to stay clean. Yours –

Slosh it 'round and spit it back out.

NOW.

Please.

SLACK
Clean?

CAMEO
Please.

5. SNAKE EYES

RO, *in other light.*

RO
The man who's picked us up drives with a broken arm. I ask if he wants to take turns and he mumbles incoherently. I've stuck Cameo in the front seat cuz, well, I'd rather him than me. It's a pickup, so I have to hide between a suitcase, under tarp, burlap, bungee-corded tight.

We stop at a casino in the armpit of the Inland Empire.

Slot machines and Russian roulette.

He says we're running outta gas money. Gave him my last envelope. From that video hustle – Hairy Gary's gone quiet. I keep the costume anyways. Makes it so strange men won't look at me strangely. Driver goes in to gamble blackjack, leaving Cam and I to fester.

CAMEO *stares inside his solo cup.*

Clipping:

CAMEO
He took the keys.

RO
I know.

CAMEO
Otherwise –

RO
Otherwise?

CAMEO
We could –

RO
No.

CAMEO
I didn't even say anything, jeez, ya don't gotta
hound me fer –

RO
If we find an opportunity, we move carefully.
Don't get all antsy for nothing.

CAMEO
This guy's a creep.

RO
The plan stays the same. We find our way south,
we hide out –

CAMEO

Violator. Violated. All whipped together. Moving southwards won't wash us of anything. No washing, not washing, not – no – no, I'm –

RO

Hey. Does your head hurt? The smell? Exhaust or something?

CAMEO

The coffee, Ro. Contain yourself.

> CAMEO *leaves, but remains in view.*

RO

Me 'n my grandmother – you'd think we were thick. La Doña. The only woman I know. Full one at least. Raised me whole. In the mornings, I am Beba. Cariña. But at night, she brands me: Perra. Cochina. To her tequila tongue I'ma symbol of dread. To her, I am jealousy manifest. Before I was born, she caught Ma playin' tonsil hockey with her boyfriend. Her boyfriend: my father. A daughter knocked up by a mother's lover, a birth, a toddler, a kidnap. La Doña takes me stateside, steals me from a family. My birthright born of spite. Sometimes I wonder, if I could go back in time, knowing what I know now, would I have volunteered myself? Rinse myself of any decision-making capability, my person, my –

I imagine it's like someone yelling: 'Hey! There's an unmarked white van outside. Waiting. Just for you. Hurry up. Jump on in.' And I do it. I jump in. It's my guiding feature. I jump, I always jump. Because it's the thing I'm told to do. And then, of course, things turn sour. Viejita finds a new man, tries to have me marry him for his papers – 'Cálmate, mija. Mira: I've given you a life of choice. I've given you opportunity. You owe me.' She says, I owed her.

A car alarm goes off.

RO
Driver's come back with a dice man – card dealer. The vest, the bowtie, the whole gig. He's got his hands all pretzel-knotted backwards, slams him on the hood. I'm impressed – broken arm and all.

SLACK
Get in the car.

RO
He takes a struggling mister casino man behind a partition and:

Time changes.

Something high pitched. Tinnitus. The smella
burning chemicals. He returns. There's no one.
Something isn't right. His face looks weathered
now. Maybe it always did.

I get in the back and we keep on down the I-15.
Driver keeps a paper package on his lap. I reach
at the sliding window, dividing front seat and
carriage. Over the wind of a speeding highway, I
scream-ask: 'Hey! What's inside that cardboard?'
He mumbles. Incoherent. I ask again: 'We good
with the money now?' More mumbles, more
fumbles.

I lay under the tarp. It crackles under the wind.
There's wind here. And the trucks in passing.
And the metal under my back. My eyes have
been kissed, closed shut. I am soft in sleep. And
in my dream, I'm somewhere ancient. Ruins
clad with vines and jungle sprawl. I see Freddy. But Freddy is my grandmother. And it's that
cornball Freddy, that Freddy fulla camp, not that
specter, not the creeper, not that monster motherfucker. I'm schoolgirl Nancy, and my grandma
Fred is coming close to me, and she's got the big-
gest fuckin' tetas you'd ever seen. Like, massive

57

breasts, growing tumorous, and they pop outta
her striped sweater and it's just two more of her,
more of him, her raisin faces staring at me, two
snake eyes slicing through me, balloons, cack-
ling, ballooning, hot.

An inflated pop.

RO
I am someone who has never been born. Someone whose death is of fantasy. And in wearing
costume, I find paradise. My paradise, making
note of a driver man playing out a history – let's
call him 'History' – my paradise, a mud spring.
Where dirt means coming back to the Earth. It
means Ampi and Hairy Gary meeting me at the
rest stop, but the rest stop is a riverbed now, and
the two of them are washing my hair, and they
like my new hat, and my skin is so clear, and
I'm awake now.

A rustle. Driver straddles CAMEO.

He's holding my baby cousin down, tryna fit a
fist in his mouth. I take my Krueger claw and
make deposit at the ankle.

Light goes red-red.

Urgent:

CAMEO
Ro, I think he's bleeding.

RO
Put him in the trunk.

CAMEO
I can't pick him up, he's too heavy, he's too –

RO
We'll take his car.

CAMEO
His arm's all fucked.

RO
Pick him up!

CAMEO
Ro, I told you, I can't!

RO
He's knocked out. Just lift him up. It's not a difficult thing.

CAMEO
Asshole pulled a tooth, my tooth, I'm –

RO
Clot the blood and cord him down. Now.

Lights relax.

We wrap the driver's ankle in a shirt. Make it so he can't move. Shoved up against the wall of the trunk, I wet a rag, I wipe his neck. I'm surprised by my own strength. Even better: I make him small. He's got this cold sweat now and part of him looks delicious. There's an itch in my throat. An itch that twists to coughing and I hacka spot of blood. I turn and Cam is staring. He looks weathered too.

When our grandmother died, Cameo, he was a bystander, a nuisance, even. From a distance we become co-conspirators. Silent agreements to hide her medicine, to stop washing, stop feeding her. At a certain point, pain proliferates into something else. Reckoning? Vengeance? When you're scared you try to relieve yourself of old habits; you turn to a timeline. You see the way it fractals and untethers from any linear. The answer's in what comes before.

Fast forward to my toaster oven, my kitchen toothbox and I – oh. I'm sorry. Sorry, wait, that's wrong. The casino. From the Inland Empire, I drink a cup of coffee. I drive the whole way south. Fifty hours straight. I don't sleep. Not for one second.

6. 404 NOT FOUND

> RO hands CAMEO a Styrofoam cup.

RO
Tómalo.

CAMEO
I don't wanna –

RO
It'll keep you awake. And while we're at it:

> She hands him a carton of –

CAMEO
Caffeine pills?

RO
Double-up.

> CAMEO takes pill, downs liquid.

RO
You're getting too close. When you get too close
you start to care too hard, and when you care too
hard you let a person take advantage. No sleep-
ing, okay? Not now. Not ever. We fall asleep,
he'll –

CAMEO
No one's touching me.

RO
–

CAMEO
You aren't well.

RO
I'm going into town. I'll sell his clothes. His car parts.

CAMEO
I can go with you.

RO
We'll make enough to stay a while.

CAMEO
Don't leave me here.

RO
Open your mouth. Let me see it.

CAMEO *opens.*

RO
No abscess. That's good. I'll get you something to sterilize. His?

CAMEO *shakes his head.*

CAMEO
Let me go with you.

> RO *puts her hand to the back of her cousin's skull.*

> *It's half inspection, half embrace.*

CAMEO
If you leave, I'll never forgive you.

RO
Is that right?

CAMEO
Maybe it's me. Maybe I'm supposed to go.

RO
You just watch him, okay?

I'll be back. I promise.

> RO *leaves,*

> SLACK *stirs.*

> CAMEO *fishes a finger in his mouth.*

> *He picks something out.*

CAMEO
My FBI agent makes a ham sandwich with mayonnaise every day, 2pm. My FBI agent is a

Jehovah's Witness with a 401k and a nice yard and laundered socks. His name is Oscar and his parents call him Junior.

Now Junior's friends with all of *your* FBI agents. They go to FBI parties on the FBI weekend, where they talk about their FBI fraternity in their FBI mansions, swimming in their FBI pools with their FBI children – 'Oh, Tina, did ya hear?' – she just had an FBI baby. She named it God. The baby is an FBI God. And I'm God. And I'm looking at you with FBI's a.k.a. 'furrowed brows incarnate,' smushing my forehead together to make you feel powerful. And my FBI agent? His CCTV gaze is a switchblade slashin' heels. He calls it his divine right. Though he forgets that I can always intercept, I can turn the camera toward him. Anyways –

I was saying: Freddy Four. The most over-produced of the franchise. Rick Johnson, the male hero, exerting his bravado by flinging nunchucks haphazardly, waiting for his boozy Pops to stumble home. Funny, the parents are always alcoholics in these movies. The salve for a collective murder – Fred Krueger, the town child-napper, serial killer, the folks of Elm

Street setting him aflame. And now boogeyman
hunts the baby-children in their sleep.

SLACK
(Full ham.) 'Christ, Cameo try to think a little
more.'

CAMEO
(Matched.) 'Yeah, I can think. I can think of how
sick I am of watching you drink your life away
and taking it out on me.'

SLACK
'Cam! Cam! I'm talking to you are you awake
or what?'

CAMEO
'Dad, don't start.'

SLACK
'Start what? Telling the little daydreamer to
wake up?'

CAMEO
The scene, underscored by Dramarama's '85 hit
'Anything, Anything.' A new wave, alt rock, cool
kid clambering. Angst. Milkshake torment. The
surrogate song of our elders. For some reason,
these old heads, they love that post punk, Mor-
rissey drawl. Robert Smith's lipstick wailing.

Likened to the corrido, the sad boy diversion, romance-ballad, a longing for home. To tell you the truth, there's something sus about it. Something like subliminal messaging, coded stimuli, telling me to get sad, to buy a sandwich, get ten credit cards, welcome my burdens. A sleight of hand. Mind control, *right?* I mean, if I begin to think of my FBI agent, Junior – imagining this guy like a pop star tricking me into allegiance, if I gift him that power – shit makes me go numb. The music, the movies, video games and tricked out cars – they're all symptoms of the scam. Diversion. Distraction. Project America.

SLACK
You like conspiracy. Both / of you.

CAMEO
It's not conspiracy.

SLACK
–

CAMEO
Sorry.

SLACK
–

CAMEO
Doesn't matter. I'ma self-surveillant. Sure. An
op dressed in radicalized sheepskin. I pick at a
bushel of virtual grapes.

SLACK
You like conspiracy 'cause it offers control.

CAMEO
–

SLACK
We're matching.

CAMEO
What.

SLACK
Bags under the eyes. Yawn adjacent.

CAMEO *sludges.*

SLACK
The clay house.

CAMEO
Right.

Between two plots, I find the thing that
cricket-shit's described. A house painted greenish-blue, hospital scrub, barred windows. A wall
topped with barbed wire and broken glass bot-

tles. Flakes of plastic-bag caught between. And, like I said, I didn't make no clay house in La Barranca. I'm *always* sure to lock the building tool. I'm suspicious, but I go inside. There's no one. Just a dusty, hollowed out twelve by twelve. A plaque of wood that says Pepsi. I try to erase the thing, but he's paralyzed my server.

The sound of Freddy's claw hand,

Dragging across metal.

CAMEO
Man –

I fucked up. Shit's frickin' humbling. A reminder: Hello! It's me! Doo-doo brain, idiot breath, waiting for some cricket-shit to come out the cut.

A metal slice.

A door creaking open.

CAMEO
I turn and fuckjob's hit his cue. In the doorway: A man. He wasn't there before. Pale-faced. A trucker hat. A shirt with the word 'Servant,' in white lettering, underscored with some Bible verse. He's a billboard for something like savior. Like those people that fly south, church group,

kids in tow, building homes, mock charity. He's
on his phone now.

SLACK *speaks as the cricket-shit:*

SLACK
'Oh *yeah*, real quaint. Took hell and a mile to get
here, though. Ten and a half Q right down the
drain. Ope, gotta go, buddy. Ride's here.'

CAMEO
He hangs up.

SLACK
'Woo-ee. Bone-tired. Made it out all this way.
Took this, uhhhh, 'tuk-tuk' from the capital,
then walked a mile or two. My baggage, my
roller bag, it's missing a wheel. Airport workers
must've – I could call and complain, but, well –
you don't care 'bout all that.'

CAMEO
Light collects. He's got burns on his face.

SLACK
'Where's *your* baggage, Cam?'

CAMEO
'What do you want?'

SLACK
'Ya like my intervention? I thought you'd 'ppreciate my keeping up with aesthetics. Y'know, the architecture – a bit *colonial*, but still got that real rustic, real exotic vibe. Yeah?'

CAMEO
'How'd you bypass my firewall?'

SLACK
'I thought we welcome guests here, no?'

CAMEO
'Who are you with? The D.O.J.? A ransomware outfit?'

SLACK
'Hold on now – '

CAMEO
'What. Do. You. Want.'

SLACK
(Laughs.) 'Want?'

CAMEO
(To audience.) My survival kit's made up of a coffee n' red bull soup. Makes me livewire. Ro says I gotta keep the eyes peeled. Lidless.

SLACK

'Ya don't look so hot. Guess I'll cut to the fix –

While I admire yer efforts toward sanctuary, the very *impressive* algorithmic skill you've displayed – I hate to disappoint you, but, we're gonna have to shut down yer lil project. Kay?'

CAMEO

'You said we'd make a deal.'

SLACK

'Ahhhh, tomato tomato tomato tomato –'

CAMEO

I wanna clock the guy. Imagine, a magnum clip, like, POW, motherfucker POW, POW. But then I hold. I, uh – I realize violence isn't tenable, and then I laugh at myself because my existence is a conjuring of something hard, ya know? Ya know? I'm the only one 'round here who knows howta circumvent a stingray. Use a scrambler hopped up on speed, fuck with police scanners – it ain't difficult. And you 'n me? What? Same swim team, different lane? I panic. La Barranca's sinking.

SLACK *as* SLACK:

SLACK
Buoyed by anonymous threats.

CAMEO
Funny thing 'bout Ro is – her birth certificate's fulla blanks. Blank time of birth, blank weight, blank name. Just, shootin' blanks.

SLACK
Name?

From the sideline:

RO
(*Chismosa.*) First name – there is none. Ro is born and Grandma's boyfriend-son-in-law-whatever – Ro's father – he tries to name her 'Veronica.' An ex-fling. Abuelita boils to the bone, she has the hospital leave it blank. Then a trend. She forces all her children to leave blanks in the paperwork of their kin. An opportunity. Notarized. A loop hole. She'll try to pass off documents as someone else's. A mill.

CAMEO
She sells mine, Ro's, our cousins' to who the fuck knows. Grandma's own little micro-economy courier service. And while she sought profit, I seek – I dunno – something else.

SLACK *as the cricket-shit:*

SLACK
'What yer doin' here ain't so – *legal.*'

CAMEO
His leather face pixels. A jaw starts to flurry –

SLACK
'A paper mill? C'mon kid.'

CAMEO
He splutters tobacco chew.

SLACK
'Runnin' a black market morgue over here – '

CAMEO
His 'Servant' shirt goes striped red 'n green, his
arms accordion out – he caught me. Crushed in
the sediment, I left text files, encrypted. Visas
and certificates, naturalizing, marriage, death
and birth alike.

SLACK
'Y'know. Ya haveta trouble the idea that you are
what you haggle.'

CAMEO
Fill in the blanks. Easy. Like learning cursive –

73

SLACK

'That yer identity – yer good will – that it's all caught up in what you got to sell. Heroes – they often look like criminals.'

CAMEO

I thought I could make it simple. Un-sniffable.

SLACK

'There are two typesa criminals in my country. The professional and the pirate. And if yer gonna stand here, hoofed down, in the shit of your own making, well – the pros – we're gonna haveta interfere.'

CAMEO

Yer frickin' history, bro.

SLACK

(Dropping cricket-shit.) Wait me? Or the other guy?

CAMEO

In poverty you aren't thinking about what mask you can try on. What wealth you can wear. You just wanna see your children. You want to eat your meals. You need to call home. And yet –

A hound sniffs out
A possum
Who cuddles

A road rabbit
Who dawdles
By the highway.

The sound of a firing shotgun.

CAMEO
Dot .net, dot .gov, dot backslash, then slash forward, then slash again. It's a brownout. Electrical power, shot. My FBI agent Junior, or cricket-shit (?), he draws his magnum clip, he makes you target practice, shoots at your haven, your router. He threatens you with an entire set of Terms and Conditions you never realized you signed off on. Ya never noticed the rule existed in the first place. A body for bodies, a country for sacrifice. I pause. I make communion with a bit of failure.

Step back.

And three, two, one.

A space bar means the death of me.

Take an EMP device and blow out cell phone contact for miles.

Kaboom.

SLACK *cowers.*

CAMEO
I've pulled the plug.

Shadowbanned from my own creation.

Everything drawn up as blank.

You erase yourself.

A web page reading: 404 Not Found.

Probably cuz you wanted to disappear in the first place.

I just wanted to appear.

SLACK
–

CAMEO
My desktop's flat-lined. Cricket-shit is gone.

SLACK
(As SLACK) I've soiled myself. Could you wipe me down?

CAMEO
Y'know, you can learn a lot from a captive's underwear. They find you, they strip you down, and that's the first insight they'll have as to how ya move about the place. Do you run or do you squirm?

SLACK
Who's they?

CAMEO
After we knock you out casino-side, we make it past Chula Vista. Ro's upset cuz our radio blows out. Cops pulled over cuz everything's static.

> *A headlight passes over everyone.*
>
> *A car door opens and slams.*
>
> *Someone holds a flashlight up to*
>
> SLACK *and* RO *and* CAMEO.
>
> *It traces over them, frozen.*
>
> *No one moves.*
>
> *Boots on gravel.*
>
> *From the side-line:*

RO
A strip search. Both of us. Underwear and beyond.

CAMEO
An excuse to see our good bits.

RO

Lucky they care for a peep show more than any
license or registration.

CAMEO

Lucky they didn't find you.

RO

Lucky, we keep driving.

> *No one moves.*
>
> *Boots on gravel.*
>
> *A car door opens and slams.*
>
> *They drive away.*

CAMEO

I'm a tighty-whitey, not a boxer brief. There a
tarot card in that?

SLACK

Yes.

CAMEO

I don't believe in all that tarot mumbo - but
you? You believe in a spliced fabric? Sacrificial
magic? That what you believe in? I would like
to know what you believe in. Please - tell me -
have faith.

Cup.

> CAMEO *takes a red solo cup from*
> *his belt.*
>
> *He shoves it in* SLACK's *face.*
>
> *A drink, a spit.*
>
> CAMEO *looks inside.*

CAMEO

That's wrong.

SLACK
Ah?

CAMEO
No. No. It's not supposed to be like this, what
did you do?

SLACK
I did exactly / what you wanted, I drink, I swirl,
I spit –

CAMEO
SHIT like SHIT like fecal-fecal SHIT, *steaming,*
steaming – a pile, a whole mangled pile of – I'm
gonna vom' all over the place, bro. All up yer
pant leg. You – you made this – there is blood
in this cup.

SLACK

Well, I don't know, man – it's your made up metric!

CAMEO

There shouldn't be blood in this cup, it should be clean it should –

The place I'm in now looks like a high school boiler room. Can't tell if I'm in video game or nightmare, or both, or in-between. A claw puckers out from beside a locker. It's her. La Doña. Eyes gone clear. Her cartoon laugh, her sentient corpse, singing her Morrisey, her New Ordered song.

SLACK

–

CAMEO

When Grandma died, Ro 'n I made a pact. We shove her inna fridge – industrial – one we keep in the garage. For months, we collect her pension. Sitting easy. No one could know.

My body's hot, Slack.

It feels like burning.

7. BROTHERLY EXCHANGE

Quiet now.

SLACK *carves a finger*

Into a finger-sized hole in the clay wall.

SLACK

A border is the fulcrum between two joining parts. Fake and not fake. Invisible 'til it's not. Monuments made in mile-high architecture. Where anachronism's common fodder. Scrap metal homes against mansions. Golf courses neighboring shanty town. Tijuana, lit up, over and over again. An itchy hole featuring bootleg indigestion.

Ope! Gotcha!

Time changes.

Something high-pitched. Tinnitus.

The view of my future's got a sticky film all over. The smella coffee beans, fruit caffeine, export hungry. A tunnel made of banana tree lacerations, a million pansy-boys, strict lines carved into their skins, their wolf hide. At the other end: spotlight. A picture of my brother. Foaming at the mouth.

From the sideline:

CAMEO *foams at the mouth.*

Time travel's a thing of spoiled fruit and barbed wire. It's juices – a potential allergen, rusted, ready to seal over, encase me, make me dead.

CAMEO *disappears.*

The sound of the shed-hole time bump.

I shake outta the wormhole and Rita-boy's gone. Lego mouth and all. Heinous. I had one job, one fruitcake job, and this idiot gets caught up in a parlor trick. I tell Crowbar Rita's missing and he freaks. I try to explain the system of these holes 'n warpings, and my brother spots a gut check.

When they're not looking, I step back to the garden shed. Touch my finger to the hole. But it's not – it won't do anything. I look back at the crusted kiddie pool, and pansy boy's still gone. Thirsty-hot in the belly, cold, sweat, my finger, where the paint pulls up, pressing harder now and the siding cuts my knuckle open. I'll trade tetanus for time, just give me time again, what's this time.

Now – I am a man-child. Assimilated by way of an American public schooling, public shootings, pop rocks, and Hanna-Barbera. I make ends meet picking up odd jobs, performing manual labor. A latchkey upbringing. Entertainment coming in things like an M-80 up a frog's ass at the nearby river bed – pop! I am the child of a tired farmhand. My father and I spoke in fragments. He'd come home covered in pesticide, wake me up for no reason, putter in my ear: *'The rule of love and labor's in both give and take.'*

Give, take. *(Realizing.)* Like clockwork, the whole thing slides into place. There's a key at my fingertip. I drive to my local hardware store, Home Depot, what have you. I call out to the day laborers, los rancheros, milling around the parking lot waiting for work. I catch one, older guy, bring him back to the kiddie pool.

(Laughs.) I can't imagine what I musta looked like, but my guy doesn't care. He sees a quick job. I see bait. 'Espérame, compa. Right here. Just a second, okay?' I do my dance. I cross to the shed. I make my tiny itch.

Boom.

We're back at it.

World Peace.

Y'know, something about the rift in time, a body can't heal and my broken arm stays broken. My mind gets a little whisked up. A patch of grass by the kiddie pool dries out. A sorta 'field of impact.' Exposure. It changes the physics of things. But the pay-off's in some morphine-ecstasy.

Back at the backyard, my ranchero, ole' Home Depot – he's gone.

Now, I spend years – years? – making exchange. Expending people. Neighbors, children, their parents, the postman. No one bats an eye since, well, there's no evidence to be found. A missing person's ad becomes the new normal, until the populace of my shitty town hits something close to zero.

Thenna couple weeks before my tooth package, I really show myself.

I call my brother to a lawn chair.

I say, 'Hey man. I love you.

And I really need to show you this thing, this thing it's –

Spectacular.

And it's really getting under my skin.'

Boom.

Whiplash.

I get thirty seconds of my brother 'n me, boys, making mud cake at the river. He puts a flower in his. I sing a song at mine. Everything smells like cinnamon.

I come back.

My brother's sent away.

Crowbar finds me sweating, half-naked. He knows. Nico Crowley Crowbar. His shoulders go un-slumped, and for the first time in my life, I realize he's five inches taller than me. He grabs at my skull, both hands the size of baseball gloves, and I think he's gonna stick his thumbs in my sockets. His nicotine breath the last stench I'll ever steal. But he pushes his face to mine. His oil patch beard. He kisses me. He leaves.

A rooster crows.

I take my toothbox, Crowley's pick-up, I drive away. Sometime soon after, I find a woman and a kid – her brother? Her lover? She looks like a fuckin' clown. I pull to the side of the road.

'Hey. Y'all need a ride?'

'I swear – I don't bite.'

8. HEAD HOLE

>>> RO *storms into space and grabs at*
>>> SLACK*'s arm.*
>>>
>>> *He tussles in pain.*

SLACK
What the hell are you –

RO
I'm resetting the elbow.

>>> *She slips his bone into place.*
>>>
>>> *He slips off his sling.*
>>>
>>> *His arm, now mobile.*

SLACK
You a ghost?

RO
A 'thank you,' maybe. Here.

>>> RO *hands* SLACK *a cardboard box.*

SLACK
Where are we?

RO
South.

SLACK
Mexico?

RO
South-er. You were knocked out. A whole week.
We'd have thought you were dead if it / weren't
for –

SLACK
A whole week?

RO
A coupla days, I don't know. Your gas ran out.
We're here now.

SLACK
Funny. That's funny.

SLACK *rotates his arm.*

RO
That way's the skirt of a village. Two miles
toward the lake. No one knows you're here, so
there's no use in making noise.

SLACK
Uncuff me.

RO
The arm should be enough.

SLACK

I'm sorry 'bout yer boy. For tryna – hustle up his mouth. I don't – I didn't mean any harm. Just – please. The cuff.

RO

No thank you.

> RO *rustles about, retrieves a cup.*
>
> *She puts it to* SLACK*'s mouth.*

RO

Drink.

> SLACK *drinks the contents of the cup,*
>
> *Holds the liquid in his mouth. Swirls.*

RO

Spit.

> *She checks her watch.*

RO

An ulcer shouldn't take so long to heal. An abscess can cause pain, fever, but you're sitting pretty. Now, what is it about a man that picks me up on the side of the road that makes me want to keep him?

SLACK

Does your head hurt, Ro?

RO

In detention they'll have you piss in a beaker.
Spit in a cup. Measure your insides to make sure
you're clean, but what's the baseline?

SLACK

I won't hurt you.

RO

There's blood falling outta my mouth. Cam's too.
Our bodies are changing, and you – your arm
stays broken. All our mouths stay red. Why is
that? Tell me. Why?

SLACK

–

RO

Go on. Grovel.

SLACK

Because we're all the same. All rotting. rotted.
Ya tú sabes.

RO

–

SLACK
–

RO

The night me n' Cam left home, a man came to visit. Grandma's latest. Boyfriend number – who cares, really. Looked like you. Imagine a man comes and wakes you up. Catches wind of our scheme. He asks for a cut of her pension.

This man's gotta shotgun habit.

Busting down the door, full-choke spray. BOOM!

Boogeyman come to get us while we sleep.

He tries to pull up on me, but remember, I've got that *shit fist*.

Tryna land him a shit-mouth.

He ducks, I miss.

Rumble backwards looking for somethin' sharp, but he's already loaded the barrel. The line of a gun pulled up to my throat.

And snap. Someone else is rolling snake eyes.

Cameo clocks the motherfucker with a hot plate. I'll never sleep again.

RO *begins to wipe away the red on her face.*

RO
I want to talk about the weather. I want to be boring. I want to tell you what book I read, what movie I saw. Let me be a freak like you carrying 'round bone-boxes. I refuse to believe that I am the person looted. I refuse to believe that I am the person looted. I refuse. I refuse to believe that I – me – that I am that person who's been, who is *being* looted. I won't expend myself for you.

SLACK
Me?

RO
Not you but – it. Them.

So you leave a place – no, not 'you' – I – me – *me* – I leave a place because I hate to imagine dying there. Dying anywhere.

And I excuse it as a way to fake my own death.

In the first Freddy, before Nancy's girl Tina gets her ass sliced open, mother says 'ya gotta cut yer fingernails or stop that dreaming.' Cochina. My nails, they fall off, uprooted from the nailbed, cuz that thing you do, that noisy thing –

I could snatch yer neck. But I won't. Yer a mascot now. History. I've claimed you.

> RO *bites at her fingernails.*

RO
The things that happen in your sleep are lost on the mind, but learned in the body.

> *She shakes her carton of caffeine pills.*

RO
You have to stay awake.

SLACK
Huh.

RO
'Huh.'

SLACK
Hate to break it to you –

> SLACK *un-pockets, shakes some pills of his own.*

SLACK
Antihistamines.

A rooster crows.

SLACK
Where's Cameo?

RO
Scrounging up a dinner freezie. Playin' computer game.

SLACK
No.

Where's Cameo?

RO *says nothing.*

SLACK
Well?

RO *begins laughing.*

SLACK
What is it?

RO
You don't – you don't *really* think –

The lights go away.

Everything is dark.

Behind the shadowed grate,

In the squared window-pit of the wall,

A screen slips on.

The metal cage unlatches.

'La Barranca.'

RO

A system restart. I turn on Cam's machine. Sticky keyboard. Boot up. A 16-bit title card: 'La Barranca'. Guess I'm finally making my appearance. It's like learning a leg or two. How to walk and how to swim. Arrow keys make it so I can run, and when I click, I drag, I change our camera view.

It's less 'themed' than expected. With a name like La Barranca, I'd assumed his fragile sense of self would decorate the place with Mayan glyphs or some bullshit. Papel Picado and fuckin' Pancho Villa. An underscore of marimba, while he whirligigs tortillas on his cock – no. It's bare. Simple. Clay, metal, ceramic, wood.

There are people here, but they can't seem to see me. I can't tell if they're visitors, props. Everyone looks like a toy figurine made of some crude wax, a gaunt impression of what they'd be in life, *Real Life*. Avatar is a shit word cuz it offers something polished. These things are fungal. Figures less like people, more like growth. I take off my shoes, or my shoes take off me, unpeeling from my foot as I step to a bank of sand.

I come upon a wood sign. A message inscribed: 'The owner of this account is dead. R-I-P. In memorium. Write a post about how sexy he is and how much you wish you could have made out with him forever and also share it on all platforms, send it to twenty contacts, or else he'll come to your bed and skin your feet and also leave pics and maybe a handle I can reach you at, I miss you, I love you, I miss you, goodnight.'

I turn. There's a clay house. It looks like this one. I peer into its window grate and see that Cam's there, talking to a wall, screaming his incel logic. Big ups to the ratboy – he's found his civic journey. I reach my hand out and it turns ten feet long. I touch a shoulder and I say, 'I'm going to swallow you whole.' I'm Fred again.

A slip and Cam is gone, as is the safehouse, and I'm plunged into the jungle thicket. I'm all knots now, cresting the edge of a riverbank, leading myself from the town center. There's an impasse. A cluster of rocks and discarded fences blocking my path. The only direction is up. I organize myself. I am my own organizing body – a hive – and I walk myself through chain link, cuz here my body imposes itself through matter. I volley myself from platform to platform, each shelf of land deeper than the last. I've reached the top of the cliffside.

I look out to a sea of gridding. Beyond the mind's eye, it's all fabricated, wireframe, virtual. There are no medics in this home. It's just me and the great testosterone burden, beveling myself against a spot of canyon. There's this ambient, ancient feeling that I'm to negotiate with someone. It reaches me like force field, retching at me: 'You're going to pay your due.'

So I dig. At the base of a wall, water and dirt. My knees caked in mud, I'm fishing, shoveling hands, fishing, and a paper emerges, cropped up in some Ziploc-plastic. My claw hands shaking, I tear it open. It's me. A picture of me. And then it quickly isn't. Is this my evolution?

Hairy Gary and I fuse together. My grandmother's scalp is my scalp, and I've got Ampi's good acrylics, but they're covering my skin like snake scale. I absorb them into my body. Look. You can see Gary's ear on my neck. Look. Cam thinks it's a 'skin tag.' I've convinced everyone it's a *skin tag*, but it's not. It's everyone made a part of me. Look. A jaw jutting out my hip bone. Look. Why aren't you looking? We've all become one moving part, and you, you'd like to trick me into believing Cam went somewhere different, when really it's all parade, and I'm just here to leech you. To make you another part of my charge.

And who swelters on the other side?

SLACK
What is it?

RO
You.

Lights fissure. Tinnitus.

CAMEO *appears.*

RO
Another world.

CAMEO
Not time travel.

RO
An explosion.

CAMEO
There was an explosion, Slack.

RO
A car exploded.

CAMEO
Crowley's pickup?

RO
It's exploding right now.

CAMEO
Bit by bit.

RO
Right in front of you.

CAMEO
That backyard?

RO
That ringing in your ears?

CAMEO
The field of impact blows you back.

RO
You bust your head –

CAMEO
The metal siding of a shed,

RO
You've crippled yourself,

CAMEO
Your arm,

RO
Your brother –

CAMEO
He's coming out of the road home

RO
He's heard a noise

CAMEO
'What's up with the gas tank,' then –

RO
Boom. Whiplash.

CAMEO
His body thrown. Landing ten, twelve feet away.

RO
You get up,

CAMEO
Ears ringing,

RO
Walk to a brother's body.

CAMEO
You flip him backwards,

RO
His teeth blown out.

CAMEO
Time travel.

RO
Crowley all gashed up the back of the skull,

CAMEO
Landed in the kiddie pool.

RO
Stirring. Ya try to feed him water from a plastic
cup,

CAMEO
But he chugs out blood.

RO
There is a ghost present.

CAMEO
Boots walking.

RO
A brother –

CAMEO
A flashlight. All of it –

RO
Tinnitus,

CAMEO
An explosion,

RO
A car,

CAMEO
A hole in the yard,

RO
A trench in the mountain,

CAMEO
No one's captured you,

RO
No Rita.

CAMEO
No Ro.

RO
No Cameo.

CAMEO
Or –

RO
Is that wrong too?

> CAMEO *goes away.*
>
> A *rooster crows.*
>
> SLACK *opens his cardboard box.*
>
> He *holds up a single tooth.*

SLACK
When I was stuck up in the pickup, after you knocked me out, you didn't notice my hip-wriggle.

I'm no expert, but I think I found my match. A vinegar package arrives at my linoleum, and finally, I understand, it's the denture of your darling. Kid cousin. Awkward by proxy.

Like – how've I gotta box of teeth? A box of *this* kid sittin' right beside me, passenger seat, full rows, a mouth that's full-on able? Remarkable, don't ya think? If there's two of him, there might be two of – I might be able to undo some things, right? Right?

RO
–

SLACK
How's yer head, Ro. I know it's been hurting.

> RO *itches at the back of her scalp.*
>
> *A look of dread.*
>
> *A scrimmage with her head-skin.*

SLACK
Take it out then.

> *One by one, from the back of her skull.*
>
> RO *pulls out four or five toy blocks,*
>
> *Wet with cartilage.*

SLACK
Lego blocks.
Pretty cool.
They can –
They, um –
Interlock,
If you're interested.

> *And then –*

SLACK
All I ask's a favor.

Reach back. Put your hand in there. You'll see a kitchen. You take this box there and you leave it on the floor. You concentrate hard enough and it'll just be me, staring at a blank wall, eating hash browns, concussive.

I won't – you just – you leave me.

You make the jump.

You can leave me there.

> *Lights out.*
>
> *A toaster oven.*
>
> *Click and ding.*

9. SOMETHING ELSE

Another day.

The face of the clay wall.

The folding chair, knocked over.

The window, repurposed.

The handcuff hangs loose at the metal grate.

CAMEO, *in other light.*

CAMEO
My utopia is one that slicks its hair back.

It shows you its face. Its lip twitches.

It's a canyon, sliced betweena jungle canopy.

There are wells of milk and honey.

Clean water – chemical free.

The view is immaculate.

Hillsides that register sunrise, sunset.

A mill of sorts.

A boot.

A car door slams.

The strike of a match.

The only trace of people you've got are in dental records.

Bone fragments. Data points.

This utopia – it might be virtual, but only because

Virtual is another word for nearly, as in almost.

My utopia – is almost.

END OF PLAY

Brutal, Horny, Stupid

In the fall of 2023, I reached out to two of my dearest friends and collaborators, writer/performer Jesús I. Valles and sound designer Michael "Stags" Costagliola. Both have had a hand in the development of 404 Not Found and I hold both as prized dramaturgs within my tight circle of peers. Turning to the digital, we held the following conversation over type:

LB: I can start by asking a very straightforward question: what do you carry from the world of this play (its people, its grammar, its logic)? What is the worth (gross: "worth") of this kind of theatre and how does it engine or excite you as a collaborator?

MC: There are images from this play I think about all the time. The grotesque ones, but tender ones too. And those are probably the most haunting. What is the worth of it? Since the pandemic began, I've heard repeated ad nauseam that audiences will be returning to the theatre for escape, for light in the dark. I don't know. I've often found myself instead wanting to stare into darkness head on, and this piece is decidedly unafraid to bring us there, and back.

JIV: I'm a sucker for a hot epigraph! Epigraphs feel so immediately like naked desire; the author saying, "This is how I want you primed for my work, how I want it framed, and what you must know before you come in here, okay?" In *404 Not Found*, Lucas, you offer this really sexy Genet quotation and then you couple it to an invocation of Lisa D'Amour as your "friend & teacher." I have always been fascinated by this move because the quotation invites us, as readers, as makers, to consider the nature of evil before we enter the work, to understand the subsequent pages, the acts in them, as an exploration of evil. At the same time, the structure of the epigraph also points to your lineage as a writer and the value of relation in your life as a writer. For me, so much of the horror in this play swirls around what we are willing to do to those we might call kin through blood, or through fraught, racial/ ethnic compulsory categorization, or through political circumstance. I'm curious about kinship, relationality, and evil in this play and what you might have to say about these things. I want to know what you think is so evil in this play, I guess! Say more about evil!

LB: Sometimes I have a hard time finding that Genet quote in print, probably because Lisa texted it to me amidst some personal-spiritual difficulty I was moving through. I think I eventually found it in an intro to *The Balcony* (don't quote me on that). Anyways, as you point out, Genet offers a bit of brutality, which is funny to hold against Lisa's teachings who—as a mentor—comes from a place of deep compassion and community-building. This might be a strange way to package evil, but I'm glad you're picking up on some clues to my subconscious. What's a simple way to describe this? Hm. Sometimes, for birthdays or holidays, I'll gift my friends switchblades with their names engraved on the handle. In its whole, I'm interested in the language of love, but I'm also interested in the threat that comes with an object's potential. Evil is something that bleeds with potential, right? When we hold a shared exposure to evil (social, economic, taxonomical, interpersonal, yadda yadda), we experience some of our greatest bonds. I mean, this play was born in the early days of Covid, when the global response to a public health crisis certainly set the tone for a Big Wickedness. Inversely, I've been on this private mission to unpack the intricacies of pity (a grandchild of pathos?), where evil can be used as a distancing technique, I think. Barthes presents pity and compassion as synonyms, used to access the fate of that ominous Other. If I hold this descriptor "evil" to the same standard, how is my sense of proximity being mangled? And then it's like, okay, we're making theatre, how does this slide into a room? I feel like my life puzzle is to unpack the question, "how do we replicate or represent evil onstage without reinforcing the grammar of it inside a collaborative process?" This feels especially pertinent coming from an artistic culture that celebrates the often diabolical auteur as visionary. But back to the play: I guess my hope is that the epigraph relieves the audience of a reading that might impose judgment. Instead, I hope we can revel in the ways transgression conditions ourselves to one another.

MC: I'm always fascinated by the idiolects you create for your characters. So much of the language in this play feels impossibly vernacular and poetic to me at the same time, especially Slack's, and I often find myself processing meaning from the lines musically rather than literally. What's your process like in creating these vocabularies? What's the balance between rulemaking and intuition?

LB: Oh man, is it boring to say the writing is mostly intuitive? I spend way too much time tweezer-ing at lines of dialogue only to satisfy what feels good in the mouth. That can make a rehearsal process a bit clenched at first, but once a performer can make the language feel at home I start to feel this incredible sensation—like a kind of hypnosis or lullaby. If I think a little more deeply about it, maybe impossibility is the pursuit. The delight of paradox? And this certainly isn't to neglect production (I feel pretty territorial thinking of my plays as plays; things to be performed for a live audience), but maybe the contradictions between an impossible language and an actualized oration becomes the solve I'm after. Maybe it mirrors the contradictions I see laden in things like character, action, plot. Like you pointed out earlier Stags, I have little patience for a language of morality or redemption in theatre. Maybe this is how I strip the need for hard meaning making and blatant resolutions? And now I'm sitting here thinking, are tongue twisters offered in our childhood as a source of play or as a source of linguistic-logical-interruption? Kidding (sort of).

JIV: Stags—may I call you "Stags?"—I'm thinking a lot about how essential design feels to this piece—how much of this play is about making, about façade and attempt, about grafting Freddy

Krueger onto ourselves, about making an else-where that is escape, even as it is doomed to be populated by nothing but us, about the sound of time travel in Slack's ears (what I always imagine as this incredibly loud nothing that leaves you unable to see). You asked Lucas about the score that language makes. I'm wondering if you might say more about your own entry into the piece. Are there any sound/scapes that feel, to you, inherently in the world of this play? I recently had my wisdom teeth removed and I stayed awake during the procedure. I was able to feel-hear the strange crunch of bone in my upper right molar as it was forced out of the bone it lived in. Right now, I can hear this laptop's age in the whir of its exhausted fan. To me, those things sound like bits of this play. I'm curious what collections of sounds feel like portals or talismans into this piece for you? What sounds conjure the nowhereness of this play?

MC: Oh those sounds are perfect. And nowhereness is exactly it too. I love Lucas's love for the nowheres and the margins. Thinking about the wind, the resonance of the deserted parking structure, the truck stop highway wash. Sound in the play is at once quotidian and a portal into the supernatural. Jesús, I love "incredibly loud nothing" for the time travel bump, you describing it that way makes me want to hear how that might translate differently in everyone's mind... in our workshop version it was this massive bass drum and a bunch of shifting sine waves at beat frequencies. The Freddy claw slice was fun too, that ended up being a combination of an ice scraper on a car windshield, chalk on chalkboard, and this screamlike cat sound. And sound here takes us to some good camp territory too, the Dramarama track and the crystalline *Nightmare on Elm Street* synths. But if I close my eyes and think about the sound of *404*, it's a rattle—that pebble in the solo cup, the wind at the chainlinks, the shoebox of teeth—sounds of brokenness in motion.

JIV: For both of you, what is it about body/horror and violence? Really, I can't stop thinking about Legos hot-glued onto gums as a horrifying mercy, about spitting into cups, and Freddy Krueger's skin. What is it about body/horror in a time of deep, observable violence?

LB: Well, it feels absolutely irresponsible to offer a play that pushes on a dramaturgy of violence without naming the myriad atrocities inflicting our collective world populace, in particular, at the very moment of writing this, the real-time genocide of the Palestinean people. I wish for a liberated Palestine now. I truly believe there is a world where this liberation can not only be found, but propagated amongst siloed peoples living thousands of miles away from one another. A freedom for one body functions as an ecosystem—a freedom for so many. But within the discourse amongst some of the more freshly radicalized, I can also hear a posturing, a "well-intentioned" public's desire to archive this pain. Turning suffering into a museum, a pat on the back for recognition alone. In the first speech of my play, Slack laughs at his given nickname, "History." It's laughable (and shattering) to antiquate live atrocity. And as a result, I find myself thinking about evisceration all of the time. It's reflexive, and part of me wishes I had a better explanation, but it feels woven into my DNA. Half of my family left Guatemala at the beginning of the country's Civil War in which an estimated 200,000 Mayan people were massacred over the 36-year period. I was born unto the dot-com boom in Silicon Valley, a region of California that has recurrently championed an excavation of land and wealth hoarding at the expense of Indigenous sovereignty and foreign laborers. At the same time, I am not the one suffering here; my histories attach me to complicit agents—the frontiersmen, the colonizers, the generally apathetic. Sometimes writing on violence feels like the only way I can try to comprehend or orient against these excessive histories. And excess is the word I would want to silo in on. I have this worksheet I offer my students when they sit to write a new play. I call it my Excess-Process pedagogical toolkit. I try to break down the steps for a writer that might call forth the density of stimuli we're all encountering, and then, wielding perception as a process of reduction or subtraction, I ask them to boil down to the essential image. Maybe that essential image is a bloodied piece of plastic. Or a kid's ingrown chest hair. Maybe this is what translates the breakdown of memory, the breakdown of the body, into newly fortified strategies of observation.

MC: I guess most of what we do is refract and reflect what's around us, right? The projection of horror into the body feels so simple and immediate and universal. This past December, I had this mystery pain in my side that came on suddenly one night and lasted a whole month, saw a bunch of doctors, bunch of tests, never got a good answer. Made me reevaluate how terrifyingly little I know about what is happening under my own skin at any given time, unlocked some new fear in that immediate ever-present unknown. I get body horror. Jesús, what does the language of the play feel like in the body as a performer? How do you approach bringing it to life?

JIV: Everyone who encounters Lucas's plays, and specifically *404 Not Found*, often comments on the quality of the language and what it asks of the actor. More than a few times, I've heard people use the words "athleticism" and "difficulty" when they speak about the piece. When I put Lucas's language in my mouth, I think about a few things: a YouTube video of Lucas reading his own work at Lambda Literary's retreat, all of the books I've seen in Lucas's Instagram stories, bookshelves, and desks, and Lucas's own encouragement to lean into stupidity and faggotry. Lucas loves words and maybe all that words can't do (there's so much they can't do!). In this play, the monologue—often seen as a luxury of lengthened speech and a captive audience—feels nothing like luxury; it feels like a desperation to be understood and to understand all that speech elides, and still, it feels like everybody knows they're bound to fail. Everyone in this play recalls a past that got them here, the architecture of potential futures that is also already poised to fail them. Speech here is like doing sped-up footage of a fox's corpse decomposing but with your mouth and it's kind of hot.

LB: Hah, I love that image.

JIV: There's this thing that happens when you're doing Lucas's language and you make eye-contact with the audience and it dawns on them, slowly, that you've just said some heinous shit, and then comes the whiplash of something deeply vulnerable, or funny, or flippant and it's disturbing—it disorients, it rearranges sense-making. As a performer, getting to drive that kind of language and land it feels so satisfying. I think doing Lucas's words makes me feel dangerous and pathetic and that's really exciting. It is already so alive on the page—it's already so ready to be brutal and unrelenting and silly. I think the best thing you can do with it is take your time to read it, then let go once it has to come out of your mouth. Think less, know more. Know nothing.

LB: Know nothing! Yes! This is reminding me of a text exchange we had after an early reading of *404*. I remember you remarked to me how horny this play is. That delighted me because 1)

I had not yet thought of it in that context and 2) I appreciated the kind of anachronistic feelings that could be invoked between those axes of the abject, the stupid, and a general faggotry.

JIV: I don't remember that text exchange at all, but I do still think this play is really horny. You name the feeling anachronistic and then I remember, of course, that I am disgusting; wretched. You insist on the sensory and the sensual throughout the play, on the body as the site of punishment and horror, on its disappearance as the only way out of a time where it might be frustratingly its worst iteration, the currency we pay to escape to time-places where people might be most themselves, makin' mud cakes. We return always to the body—a Lego piece in the back of the neck, maybe. In this play, the body feels as a machine that only serves to satiate its dumb hungers and does so poorly with the strangest concoctions. Everybody in this play wants too hard, so wickedly, often at great and horrifying costs. That's really horny to me, I think. Everybody is so stupidly criminal, which is the most Genet kind of horny you could be. Frustrating want is a horny thing, and rushing to its satisfaction is heartbreakingly horny, too. And still, there's nothing sexy here. Being horny is seldom sexy. Being horny is mostly stupid and sad, so the play is horny. At times, this play smells like a truck-stop bathroom, or a stranger's shitty room during a 4 am hook up, a mattress on the floor with dubious specks of life on them. Again, I am disgusting, and maybe so is this play. I think a lot about you telling me in a workshop that Slack is a faggot and how much that particular revelation opened for me about how to move into those moments that felt like they were desperate with this wanting to be with—with Cameo, with Rita-boy, with his brother. Yeah, horny makes sense. Horny's right.

MC: Okay, Lucas wrote "Stags, do you have feelings re: horniness" in this part of the Google Doc and how do I dodge that? Jesús, I think that polarity between horny and sexy is so important here—I remember when *Eyes Wide Shut* came out everyone was talking about it like it was this sexy erotic odyssey and I remember watching it and thinking how unsexy it was, but rather, it's Tom Cruise wandering around New York with the sort of one-sided desperate horniness of a fifteen-year-old boy who has never had a conversation with a woman. There's this unique intersection of desperation and boredom in the word horny, and that's Slack—horny thumb, horny time-shed-hole of deliverance. Also it feels like the only character who approaches an understanding of their sexuality is Ro, and it's a shell that's replaced with violence, a heimlich maneuver. Okay Lucas? Um, delete this if you want.

LB: No, no, that definitely feels true. Maybe if it's not a complete understanding, Ro knows how to best compartmentalize her desire. Maybe that's a mechanism for survival. Okay, wait, but I have a complete tangent. As I'm thinking about horniness as a hallmark of the play, I'm also thinking about time—of course, as this narrative piece, but also as a value held up in the making of the work. Stags, I remember the first time we workshopped this play with the Kennedy Center, it was also the first time we worked together. You were quick to take on a generative role with the actors as they read text. I was impressed by the speed at which you could deliver such quality, lived-in sound. Do you find that strict time parameters in a process like ours end up helping you creatively? In creating a sense of urgency? Does it change from project to project? What does it do to the spirit of your work?

MC: Strict time parameters are why I do theatre. For real. Without the threat of opening night I'd never get anything done. As a freelancer, it's rare that I'm brought on to projects early enough to participate when they're still in a generative phase, but I have so much more fun when it happens. Or when I get to work on devised pieces. I'm not a jazz musician but I've forever been fascinated with the mechanics of jazz improvisation, and a yearslong project of mine has been creating a sandbox setup for myself where I can respond sonically to performers in a rehearsal room at the same speed they're responding to each other. Where I don't have time enough to think, only react emotionally. Right now that setup is an unholy mess (Max/MSP, Logic, and Ableton criss-crossed together) but it works. And if I can get to that kind of flow state, I often make more interesting choices than if I have time to analyze, and can get into a conversation with a performer where we're feeding off each other. I remember that happening a couple times in our first workshop and it's a holy grail kind of feeling for me in a process.

LB: I also wanted to tell you that I'm taking this virtual sound studies class right now. Well, it's a reading group, I guess. I feel a bit out of my element, but I'm excited by the way these musicians and academics and other sound people are thinking about a distinction between "hearing" and "listening" (a physiological experience vs a psychological one). I wonder, when confronted with a text that might necessitate a more active ear, what invites you in and what alienates you? Is there room for an ambient hearing versus an active listening?

MC: I have a note on my phone called "Quotes" that consists primarily of dumb things my friends have said over the years but also my favorite bit from John Cage: "Wherever we are, what we hear is mostly noise. When we ignore it, it disturbs us. When we listen to it, we find it fascinating." I'm constantly thinking about this. And I don't think what he calls being "disturbed" is always a negative. I think there's so much power in a sensation that's felt instead of comprehended, and I love to work in that territory when I'm creating soundscapes, especially ones that need to coexist with text. Like I was saying before with the musicality of your characters' speech, I love scoring to your text, because like a well-written song, I think it regularly operates in both these registers—you can let it wash over you and it's good music, or you can dive in deep and it's "disturbing" on a totally different level.

JIV: After the first reading I watched, I was so, so, so entranced with Ro. Like every proper trans-border Mexican subject, I have a deep love for horror and a childhood fascination with Freddy Kreuger. I found J.T. Leroy's *Sarah* in 9th grade and learned the term "lot lizard" there; I wanted to be one so desperately. I also just hung out with a bunch of cholitas and goth girls in middle school, so Ro was so immediately dazzling to me, with that mean prima energy. Ro is a chimera made of all the things maladapted queers might desire to be most; powerful, terrifying, willful. As an audience member, I left with Ro. I snuck her out as a figure to pin up on the inside of my high school locker, a magazine cutout of someone I want to be on my vanity.

LB: God, yeah, so much to say on the cholita-cochina amalgam. On the Mexican side of my family, I've always been equally entranced with the relationships between my mom and her sisters. They're a real wiley crew. They'd show up on weekends unannounced from L.A. to cram into our small house in San Francisco. They reminded me of the girls from *Mi Vida Loca*, but even in saying that I know they would reject the whole "chola" label. There's a lot of love there, but they're also big grudge-holders. I've probably inherited that soup. These relationships once removed (aunts, cousins, grandparents and their grandchildren) keep cropping up in my writing, I think, because it feels like there are no predetermined social rules for how those kinds of relations are supposed to function. Everyone's on the defense or sitting inside some sort of survival hustle.

JIV: Then, I did the reading and that fucked me up. The logics of the time travel mechanism you invented, its crass transaction and how quickly its pleasure seemed to flee, how addictive it feels to regress, and what we're willing to sacrifice for this fix—god, even responding to this, I want it so bad. I want it so bad! I want it so bad. I want to not be here so bad. I want to itch the corner of some shed and be away and be gone and be smaller than I am, somewhere else. I want morphine-ecstasy. I want how much I want to feel good to slowly end everything around me until I'm gone, too. Maybe I want to sit on that lawn chair and have someone be rid of me, too. I want to be a time token. I walked away from participating in that reading thinking about how much it broke my heart for Slack to "really show [him-self.]" Here are the most heartbreaking lines of this play for me:

SLACK
"I call my brother to a lawn chair.
I say, 'Hey man. I love you.
And I really need to show you this thing, this thing it's—
Spectacular.
And it's really getting under my skin.'
Boom.
Whiplash.
I get thirty seconds of my brother 'n me, boys, making mud cake at the river. He puts a flower in his. I sing a song at mine. Everything smells like cinnamon.
I come back.
My brother's sent away."

I remember sitting with these lines, thinking about your own brothers, Lucas, thinking about mine, and choking up at the rehearsal table. I measured the strange distance between deportation and citizenship, and how that, too, is a kind of time travel. I missed my brother, who is an asshole. Mostly, I felt for Slack. I felt for the loss experienced in this fiction, and the pleasure that loss promises. I think it's maybe the most beautiful piece of text I've ever performed. That's not blowing smoke up your ass. I truly mean it's so delicate, and brutal, and gorgeous to long for an impossible boyhood next to someone we want to love and suddenly they're gone. Pleasure is such a doomed project under colonization. We're so doomed. Lol.

LB: First, to acknowledge that desire to disappear: if I outline the very essential desires of these three characters, I think it's what they all want. To rid themselves of something. And that passage you point to—it feels like the core of the play. Masculinity is the site of complete failure. These bespoke relationships with brothers, and by extension, machismo, certainly make me feel some brand of grief. Maybe that's why representations of an abject queerness have always felt correct to me. Horror has been a salve because I can hold it up against my own navigation of pain. Jesús, I think about your play *(Un)Documents* and your figure of a brother removed. I have four brothers and sometimes some of them are assholes like yours, but also sometimes I'm the asshole. Sometimes I feel so distant from them and tethered at the same time. Sometimes I want to be closer and sometimes I cherish the vise grip I hold over my private life. You're right to note the pleasure that can surface inside this flavor of self-flagellation. Makes it easier to both narrativize the unremarkable things in my life and tame the brutality of the world. As for the time mechanic, I owe a shoutout to Alexander de Vasconçelos Matos (who originated the role of Cameo) for putting me onto the anime *Fullmetal Alchemist* and its presentation of transmutation as a concept of physical exchange. Funny, there's also a lot of brotherly-sacrifice drama in that show. Real cornball shit.

MC: Lucas, I remember talking to you early on in the Kennedy Center process about recurring nightmares you had towards the beginning of the pandemic, something I experienced too. How much of those dreams informed your writing process? Is your subconscious a place you find useful to mine creatively? Still ever have those nightmares?

LB: I have such poor sleep hygiene. I sleep next to my phone. Because of this, sometimes I'll wake up in the middle of the night and when I have a super active dream I'll jot down a note in a text message to myself. Often I'll wake up the next morning to read complete gibberish, but pieces of dreams do end up in my plays. Nowadays it's hard to discern between those dreams and nightmares. It all holds a kind of discomfort. And the recurring things—the apocalypses, the chases, the Freddy encounters, getting shot— they're all still there. A recent image repetition of the last several years is this final moment in my dreams where I come upon a person with their back toward me. They turn around and it's me. I'm grinning at myself. And then I wake up. Reminds me of this Levinas quote I have stickered over my desk: "[S]leep is always on the verge of waking up...sleep remains attentive to the wakefulness that threatens it."

MC: What is it about time travel?

JIV: Who wants to be here now? The settler-colonial present is an always death project. The "here and now" is always an attempt to look away in order to avoid the risk of remembering. The here and now is an attempt to stifle all the things your bones already know are coming. It's infuriating to be "here"—I hate it here. I think time travel is a technology of longing (I certainly don't want to go to the future). I hate right now, so time travel is a technology of escape ("now" is devastating). The future looks bleak, too. Here we are, nonetheless, in our little fleshy time-machines, remembering all the times, projecting a tomorrow, a next year. It's already too late. I understand the obsession with it, its allure.

LB: I'm going to sound like a real freak for a second, so be patient. If I propose that linearity is a human evaluation—one based on entropy, orbit, religion, agriculture—then maybe, is there a liberated perspective in which we're always time traveling? I remember reading Heriberto Yépez for the first time when I was sitting on a balcony in San Lucas Tolimán five years ago. Yépez taught me the concept of Kinh, the Mayan belief that time is spatialized, that time is an ecosystem. Inversely, the "time" we seek out in the U.S., in a contemporary work life, bound to capitalism and embraced familial structures and hetero-normative pathways—it becomes an exercise in artifice. Yépez says, "[T]here is no history that does not mutate into apocrypha." The mutation of memory is inevitable. The formation of new memory or a new system of remembering is inevitable. Nostalgia is a kind of iconoclasm, but it's happening so slowly that it's hard to trace. By socializing physics, we're weaving little lies into ourselves every day. The lies then have the opportunity to either champion the linear or fork our pathways. Isn't that beautiful? Hah.

This is definitely my own escapist practice, but it's all just theatre, no?

'EXCESS' AS A GENERATIVE // PEDAGOGICAL TOOL

Loitering –

From Lewis Hyde's *Trickster Makes This World*. Where is the imp-writer and how do they navigate some middle space between gift and theft? These are the primary tenets of every trickster story, across cultures. Where are the places that you, the imp-writer, can wait and wander? What about these places delights you, encourages something desirous? Where do you 'not belong' and (without completely affixing yourself) how can you try to make shelter? What are you not allowed to hold? How can you try to hold it?

Forensics –

Who are the ghosts you're trying to follow? How can you utilize a forensic gaze to coax out said ghosts? Technologies may include: the site visit, audio recording, photojournalism, access to archive. As you pilfer, where do you allocate moral truths and find accepted falsehoods? What does a backwards sense of *justice* look like? A forward one? Where are there patterns? How have you evaluated (or willfully misinterpreted) all of your 'evidence?' What is your most sideways version of research?

Deluge –

The great flood washes out entire continents. You're left with five or six bones of your collecting and research. Spew it back out at the word processor. If 'canon' translates to a 'rule of faith,' what does your writing believe in? What's been vandalized and what's been kept pristine? How has a food chain structured itself, and how has it adapted? What layers on top of // beneath // beside other layers? What does your writing long for that it has lost?

Metabolism –

The body has synthesized your writing as cellular data, converting it into a play, or general 'play,' with its own biological intentions. It suggests a roadmap. Something chiseled, yet permeable. Something in it's code suggests an origin of life. Thematic breakages and attachments are left to your reader's discretion. Your collaborators must agitate *with* the language.

Acknowledgments

First, I want to thank Kate Kremer and Nathan Baron Silvern at 53rd State Press for making this book happen. Beyond this project, your care and your faith are invaluable forces within our community.

Thank you to Gregg Henry at the Kennedy Center, as well as the National New Play Network, who gave this play its first home. 404 wouldn't exist without those initial workshops. Thank you to the Princess Grace Foundation, The Tank, and more specifically, Emily Morse, John Steber, and Tyler Christie at New Dramatists for hosting the first public presentation of this work. Thank you to all the directors, actors, dramaturgs, and designers who have lifted these pages into existence: Nicole A. Watson, Martine Kei Green-Rogers, Daniel Duque-Estrada, María Gabriela González, Alexander De Vasconçelos Matos, Michael Costagliola, Amauta Marston-Firmino, Adil Mansoor, Fernando Gonzalez, Cat Rodríguez, and Jesús I. Valles.

Thank you to my fellow artists-in-residence at The Helene Wurlitzer Foundation, Millay Arts, and Page 73 with whom I shared the strangest of drafts. Thank you to the Jerome Foundation and all of you Minneapolis folk who kept me up while the cold kept me down: Zola Dee, Rachel Jendrzejewski, Sarah Meyers, and Dylan Nesser (your gifts of books are always welcome).

A tremendous thank you to my intrepid family of writerly friends who share with me the great burden and bliss, the trials of making: Imani Elizabeth Jackson, Danny Epstein, Emma Horwitz, Julia Izumi, Noah Diaz, Noah Weinman, Sam Max, Quetzal Maucci, Ida Cuttler, Kajsalena Benrubi Seagrave, Theadora Walsh, Ryan Drake, and Bailey Williams. I'm grateful that I can reach forward to each of you when that work light feels dim.

Thank you to my artistic heroes for encouraging an expansive practice that includes rigor, pain, and play: Dennis Cooper, Ian Cheng, Roberto Bolaño, Jean Genet, Ursula K. Le Guin, Mariano Pensotti, Hito Steyerl, and Heriberto Yépez.

I thank my students for holding me accountable. I thank my teachers past and present, those who equipped me, taught me kindness, taught me a critical dramaturgy: Lisa D'Amour, Julia Jarcho, Dean Corrin, Bonnie Metzgar, Geoffrey Jackson Scott, Erik Ehn, and Phillip Rayher.

Thank you to California, always. Thank you to Lake Atitlán.

Thank you to JessicaLight, the teacher from New York who would help my brother Jesse and I grind MMORPG campaigns at 1 am Pacific time. Two decades ago, you made the Internet something to be less afraid of. I hope you're doing okay.

Thank you to Phongtorn Phongluantum, my old boss from my days working at the MCA Chicago. Thank you for all those meals, Torn. Thank you for the conversation. Thank you for giving me the time of day.

And lastly, thank you Wes Craven and Robert Englund. Freddy has nestled himself into my subconscious for the last twenty-five years. Your haunting is what made this whole play a problem to decipher in the first place.

Contributors

Lucas Baisch is a playwright, artist, and educator from San Francisco. His plays have been read and developed at the Goodman Theatre, The Playwrights' Center, The Bushwick Starr, The Mercury Store, First Floor Theater, Cutting Ball, Playwrights Horizons, Clubbed Thumb, The Neo-Futurists, Chicago Dramatists, Links Hall, etc. Lucas is a recipient of a Steinberg Playwright Award, the Princess Grace Award in Playwriting, a Jerome Fellowship, the Kennedy Center's KCACTF Latinx Playwriting Award, and the Chesley/Bumbalo Playwriting Award. Outside of writing for theatre, his artwork has been presented at Elsewhere Museum, the Electronic Literature Organization, gallery no one, and the RISD Museum. He has held residencies through Ars Nova, Elsewhere Museum, Page 73, the Lower Manhattan Cultural Council, the Djerassi Resident Artists Program, Millay Arts, ACRE, the Helene Wurlitzer Foundation, the Goodman Theatre's Playwrights Unit, and as a Lambda Literary Playwriting Fellow. Lucas's previously published plays include *Dry Swallow* (Bloomsbury/Methuen Drama) and *On the Y-Axis*

(Yale's Theater Magazine). He received his MFA in Playwriting from Brown University.

Michael Costagliola is a New York-based sound designer and composer. His work has been heard in New York in productions by The Public, New York Theatre Workshop, La MaMa, Page 73, Rattlestick, and Ars Nova among others, as well as regionally at Shakespeare Theatre Company, Two River Theater, Yale Rep, Alabama Shakespeare Festival, St. Louis Rep, and at various other theaters across the U.S. and abroad. AB in Music from Brown University, MFA in Sound Design from Yale School of Drama.

Jonathan Herrera Soto (b. 1994, Chicago) lives and works in New Haven, CT. He received an MFA from The Yale School of Art in Painting & Printmaking and a BFA from Minneapolis College of Art and Design. Solo exhibitions of Herrera Soto's work include "In Between / Underneath" at the Minneapolis Institute of Art and "All at Once" at Cohen Gallery, Brown University. He recently received the Yale Prison Education Initiative Fellowship, Jerome Hill Artist Fellowship, Paul and Daisy Soros Fellowship, and was the 2023-2024 Koopman

Distinguished Chair in the Visual Arts at the Hartford Art School.

Julia Jarcho is a playwright and director with the NYC company Minor Theater. Her plays include *Grimly Handsome* (2013; OBIE), *Every Angel Is Brutal* (2016), *Pathetic* (2019), and *Marie It's Time* (2022). She has also written two scholarly books: *Writing and the Modern Stage: Theater Beyond Drama* (Cambridge, 2017) and *Throw Yourself Away: Writing and Masochism* (forthcoming from University of Chicago Press). She's the head of playwriting at Brown.

Jesús I. Valles is a Mexican writer-performer who wishes to echo Rasha Abdulhadi's call to you, dear reader, to refuse and resist the genocide of Palestinian people. "Wherever you are, whatever sand you can throw on the gears of genocide, do it now. The elimination of the Palestinian people is not inevitable. We can refuse with our every breath and action. We must." Our liberation is bound to one another. May every border end.

53rd State Press publishes lucid, challenging, and lively new writing for performance. Our catalog includes new plays as well as scores and notations for interdisciplinary performance, graphic adaptations, and essays on theater and dance. 53rd State Press was founded in 2007 by Karinne Keithley. In 2017, Kate Kremer took on the leadership of the volunteer editorial collective. For more information or to order books, please visit 53rdstatepress.org.

53rd State Press books are represented to the trade by TCG (Theatre Communications Group). TCG books are exclusively distributed to the book trade by Consortium Book Sales and Distribution, an Ingram Brand.

LAND & LABOR ACKNOWLEDGMENTS
53rd State Press recognizes that much of the work we publish was first developed and performed on the unceded lands of the Lenape and Canarsie communities. Our books are stored on and shipped from the unceded lands of the Chickasaw, Cherokee, Shawnee, and Yuchi communities. The work that we do draws on natural resources that members of the Indigenous Diaspora have led the way in protecting and caretaking. We are grateful to these Indigenous communities, and commit to supporting Indigenous-led movements working to undo the harms of colonization.

As a press devoted to preserving the ephemeral experiments of the contemporary avant-garde, we recognize with great reverence the work of radical BIPOC artists whose (often uncompensated) experiments have been subject to erasure, appropriation, marginalization, and theft. We commit to amplifying the revolutionary experiments of earlier generations of BIPOC theatermakers, and to publishing, promoting, celebrating, and compensating the BIPOC playwrights and performers revolutionizing the field today.

404 Not Found is made possible by the New York State Council on the Arts with the support of the Office of the Governor and the New York State Legislature.